You & Me LORD

Study Guide and Leaders Notes

Author: Carolyn Sims
Editor: Carolyn Bergt
International Lutheran Women's Missionary League Consultant: Carol Zehnder

CPH
SAINT LOUIS

Acknowledgment

The International Lutheran Women's Missionary League Christian Growth Committee has consulted with the editor and author in the development of this Bible study, and recommends its use.

3558 S. Jefferson Avenue
St. Louis, MO 63118-3968
Manufactured in the United States of America

1 2 3 4 5 6 7 8 9 10 05 04 03 02 01 00 99 98 97 96

Contents

Study Guide

Leaders Notes

Introduction

You are invited to spend time in the light of God's Word, looking at some of the challenges we face in our lives today. Whether these challenges appear as positives or negatives, the bottom line is that we are not facing them alone—it's "You and Me, Lord" together. If you are needing support and encouragement, or if you are someone the Lord can use to support and encourage someone else, you will be reminded again and again in these pages of God's great blessings as He offers *Pardon for the Past, Power for the Present,* and *Promise for the Future.* Let the song "God Is with Me" be your theme song of praise for God's constant strength and presence in your life.

SESSION 1

You and Me, Lord, ...

as I experience brokenness caused by sin!

Reflection: "Fix It, Please!"

The distraught child runs to her father's waiting arms, clutching the pieces of a broken toy. "Fix it, please!" she sobs, handing him the disjointed parts and peering expectantly through the tears into his sympathetic eyes. It seems to little children that moms and dads can fix anything. A broken wagon? Daddy can fix it. A torn picture? Get Mom and her roll of tape. A broken heart? That's more difficult.

One of the passages from childhood into adulthood is the realization that there are some things in life which appear to be unfixable; some decisions whose consequences cannot be set aside; some hurts that no amount of kisses and bandages can heal.

What is broken in your life today? What do you bring to your heavenly Father for repair as you proceed with openness to His precious Word for you? Pray together with the psalmist these words of healing and wholeness.

Psalm 51—A Paraphrase

O God, may the measure of Your eternal love be the measure of Your mercy. ...

I have failed, O Lord, and my failures weigh heavily upon my heart. ...

You know what they are, O God, and how far I have fallen short of Your standards and expectations. ...

The weaknesses that plague me are not all of my doing, nor can I handle them by my strength alone. ...

I can only acknowledge my indictment and accept Your loving forgiveness.

Purge me of my guilt, O Lord; heal the hurts of those who have been afflicted by my failures. ...
Restore to me the joy and assurance of a right relationship with You. ...
It is only then that my tongue will be set free to sing Your praises
And my hands to perform the tasks You have set before me. ...
I do come to You with a sincere desire to be Your servant,
To walk in Your course for my life,
To receive Your love and share it with [people] about me.
I thank You, God, that this is acceptable to You
And that I will remain Your [child] forever. Amen.

From *Psalms/Now,* by Leslie Brandt. © 1973 CPH.

Pardon for the Past

For something to be broken implies that it was once together. For something to be fixed, one must first determine the location of the damage. Let's take a look at some of the broken strands that may occur in our lives and trace them back to their beginnings.

1. List examples of brokenness that you have seen or known.

Broken Promises:

Broken Dreams:

Broken Relationships:

Broken Families:

Broken Marriages:

Broken Hearts:

2. Now find these examples in Scripture of people who experienced the same brokenness. Match the Bible reference to the type of broken strand listed.

___ Genesis 27:41–45	a. Broken Promises
___ Luke 22:33–34, 55–62	b. Broken Dreams
___ 2 Samuel 11:2–5	c. Broken Relationships
___ 2 Samuel 18:33	d. Broken Families
___ Genesis 37:5–8, 26–28	e. Broken Marriages
___ Genesis 3:8–10	f. Broken Hearts

3. What do all these examples have in common? What one factor is the cause of all this pain? What is the basic break that needs to be repaired before anyone or anything can be really whole again? Romans 5:12 and 7:5 provide the answer.

When sin entered the world, the wholeness God had planned for His people shattered into the jagged fragments of pain, fear, sorrow, and death. As Adam and Eve realized what they had done, they were defenseless in the face of the overwhelming damage they had caused. (Have you ever felt a similar sense of despair?) As they listened to God's voice of wrath, they knew that nothing would ever be the same again. The world and everything in it was ruined.

But, while Adam and Eve were still grieving over what they had broken, God had already begun to fix it.

Power for the Present

Let's take a closer look at those broken strands and how God alone can put them all together again.

1. It is true that sin separates us from God. But while that sin may break God's heart, it does not destroy His love for us. As God surveyed the brokenness caused by sin, He immediately promised to repair the damage. What is the picture of salvation portrayed in Genesis 3:15? Draw or describe it.

In this verse, God is speaking to the devil, who has taken on the form of a serpent in order to tempt Adam and Eve. The seed, or offspring, of Adam and Eve would be Jesus. He would crush the power of Satan and would die in the process. Read Revelation 12:9–10 for a description of how God's repair job will look for all eternity.

2. In the meantime, we are living with the frayed ends of reality in a world that doesn't know it has been fixed. Even now, we see God at work putting the pieces back together in two significant ways.

   First, He restored the relationship between Himself and us through Jesus' death on the cross and resurrection from the grave. Jesus satisfied God's judgment, made us one with God again, and healed the broken relationship severed by sin. The title of this Bible study series—*You and Me, Lord*—reflects this miracle of reconciliation. If it were not for Jesus, there would be no connection. Our title would have to read, *Me against You, Lord.* And there is no doubt about the result of such a confrontation—it would be a short, sad story.

   The incredible fact is that God has chosen to link Himself to us for all eternity through the strong, unbreakable bond of His love for us in Christ Jesus. Though sin once separated us from God, of what are we assured in Romans 8:38–39?

3. The other facet of God's restoring hand is that He is with us even in our disrepair. We experience the consequences of sin in this world. We live with broken dreams, broken promises, and broken relationships. But we have a Father to whom we can bring our pieces and our prayers with the entreaty, "Fix it, please."

   Scripture is full of examples of people who were broken in one way or another, but who were restored by God to serve Him in spite of their weaknesses. In fact, notice how often God makes the best use of their very weakness.

   Read about each of the following people, find their areas of brokenness, and indicate how God used them to carry out His will.

	Brokenness	**Blessing**
Moses (Exodus 4:10–12; 33:7–11a)		
Samson (Judges 16:15–19, 28–30)		
Rahab (Joshua 2:1–21; Matthew 1:5–6)		

	Brokenness	Blessing
Hannah (1 Samuel 1:1–20; 2:1–8, 21)		
The Blind Man (John 9:1–12, 28–38)		
Paul (Acts 9:1–22)		
You (Romans 8:18, 26, 28)		

4. God provides the resources to build us up in times of brokenness. What are some of the contents of His "repair kit"?
   a. Philippians 4:6 ______________________________
   b. Psalm 119:105 ______________________________
   c. Matthew 26:26–28 ___________________________
   d. Ecclesiastes 4:9–12 _________________________
   e. Luke 7:41–50 _______________________________
   f. Isaiah 12:2 _________________________________
   g. Romans 6:3–4 ______________________________
5. Which of the following responses best demonstrate how you feel about using the resources in God's "repair kit" in your own life?
   I. When it comes to prayer,
      a. I always use it as a last resort.
      b. God helps those who help themselves.
      c. I don't like to bother God with trivial matters.
      d. I can rely on it in every circumstance.
   II. My Bible
      a. is something I used to read.
      b. contains some interesting stories.
      c. helps me understand myself and others better.
      d. shows me God's will for my life.

III. When I partake of the Lord's Supper,
   a. I am afraid I am not worthy.
   b. I try hard to look pious.
   c. I wish I felt more at peace.
   d. I am assured of God's forgiveness and strength.

IV. My Christian friends
   a. can be a real pain sometimes.
   b. just don't understand me.
   c. are too critical.
   d. are there to support and comfort me.

V. When it comes to forgiveness,
   a. I can receive it, but I can't give it.
   b. I can give it, but it's hard for me to feel forgiven myself.
   c. I can forgive, but I can't forget.
   d. I am able to forgive others because I know God has forgiven me.

VI. Trust means:
   a. Try not to worry.
   b. Always work with a safety net.
   c. Hold on and hope.
   d. Let go.

VII. My Baptism
   a. is just something in my past.
   b. is a tradition in our church.
   c. is something I haven't thought about lately.
   d. is one of the means of grace through which God has given me forgiveness and the new life I now live in Christ.

VIII. The best thing about God's repair kit is:
   a. It is always open.
   b. The tools are always sharp.
   c. He supplies the power.
   d. It has my name on it.

Promise for the Future

1. Think of one thing that is broken in your life right now. How does the fact that you are a redeemed child of God affect that situation? How will you make use of the tools God provides to bring about healing and restoration?

2. Sometimes others may come to you with fragments of their lives in their hands and beg, "Fix it, please." Who looks to you as a source of strength and support? In the following list put a star in front of those who are easy to help; put a check mark in front those who are more difficult for you to serve.

___ my children	___ people of my race
___ my spouse	___ people in prison
___ my neighbor	___ homeless families
___ my other neighbor	___ homeless men
___ battered women	___ unwed mothers
___ batterers	___ church members
___ myself	___ ________________

Consider: What makes it harder to help some people than others? Is their need different, or is your attitude toward them different?

3. Read Ephesians 2:13–22. Here is God's promise for the future. It pictures separated people brought together by the love of Christ, broken people put back together by the power of His grace, disjointed relationships held together by the bond of His mercy.

   What is the result? Look again at verse 17. Christ converts pieces into peace, hostility into wholeness, foreigners into family. He holds the broken fragments of our lives together and does more than fix them; He fuses them into something even better than before—His new creation, flawless, the image of His whole and perfect Son.

4. The psalmist reminds us that God loves broken people. In fact, according to Psalm 51:17, what does God desire?

We would ordinarily be upset if we opened a gift that was broken. But a broken and contrite heart is the kind of heart God knows we need. A broken spirit and a contrite heart, by the power of the Holy Spirit, looks to Jesus for fixing. When a person breaks an arm or leg, the pain is excruciating. Getting help is the top priority. Nothing else matters until relief is achieved. So our brokenness drives us to Jesus for comfort and healing. As we cry, "Lord, fix it, please!" He welcomes us with a smile and says, "I already have."

Certainty

Our lives are broken by sin—both that of our own doing and that of others. While we must live with the consequences of sin in this world, the damage is not irreversible. Jesus' death for us on the cross restored our relationship with God. Now nothing can break that relationship. Christ comforts and sustains us in our times of trouble and renews us to do His will.

Prayer

Pray silently for God's help for the brokenness you have experienced or are experiencing. Thank God for His healing and restoring power. Then pray or sing together this stanza of "Today Your Mercy Calls Us" (*LW* 347).

Today your gate is open, And all who enter in
  Shall find a Father's welcome And pardon for their sin.
The *past* shall be forgotten, A *present* joy be giv'n,
  A *future* grace be promised, A glorious crown in heav'n.

You and Me, Lord, ...

as I become physically tired!

Reflection: Catching Your Second Wind

Shawna landed with a thud as she catapulted from the swing. Her mother asked with concern, "Are you okay?"

After an agonizing 10 seconds, Shawna managed a husky reply, "Yes, ... I just had the wind knocked out of me."

Have you ever experienced that sensation? The air rushes out of your lungs and your whole body goes into suspension until you are replenished with life-sustaining oxygen.

Sometimes we feel like we are suffocating physically. After a traumatic occurrence or as a result of the buildup of sustained physical strain, we feel totally depleted. We feel incapable of functioning—at least for a little while—until we catch our breath once more.

The psalmist also felt exhaustion. Pray with him now for a second wind to sustain you through this day.

Psalm 17—A Paraphrase

I cry to You out of desperation, my God. ...

I am tripped up by despair.

There are great walls that I cannot break through, dead ends that lead nowhere, people to whom I cannot relate. ...

I am weary, Lord, weary of well-doing. I am tired of the reactions of those I seek to serve. I seriously wonder if it is all worth it.

Grant me, O God, a measure of ecstasy. Help me feel good about myself and about my role in Your service.

Reveal Yourself in some special way ... that I may rest in joy and peace. Amen.

From *Psalms/Now*, by Leslie Brandt. ©1973 CPH.

Pardon for the Past

1. Our modern age, with its labor-saving devices, makes it possible for us to work at home and at the office, in the yard or in the car, any time of the day or night. The natural result of all that busyness is physical fatigue. What kinds of activities make you the most tired? Rank the jobs listed below in the order in which you find them the most physically draining, starting with "1" as the task that makes you the most tired.

   ____ Yardwork
   ____ Organizing closets
   ____ Writing letters
   ____ Cleaning the house
   ____ Dealing with finances
   ____ Shopping
   ____ Keeping up with social demands
   ____ Taking care of laundry
   ____ Pressures on the job
   ____ Chauffeuring the family here and there
   ____ Decorating for a party
   ____ Attending meetings
   ____ ____________________________
   ____ ____________________________

   Is it always the job requiring the most physical activity that tires you the most? What other factors could be at work in determining how much fatigue you feel?

2. When children start to whine or lose patience, we immediately know they need some rest. What are you like when you are tired? Can others tell, or do you keep your feelings hidden? List some words that describe you when you need rest:

   The obvious solution is that when you feel tired, you need to sleep. But taking time for proper rest isn't always as easy at it seems. People often think of sleep as something that is a necessary evil, an activity to be avoided as long as possible while you work a little longer, and then indulged in only briefly. Taking a nap or relaxing break seems so irresponsible when there is so much to do. The truth is, getting enough rest is one of the most responsible things we can do for our bodies and minds.

Take this "Sleep Quiz" to assess your knowledge about this magnificent gift from God. Indicate whether you believe each statement is true or false.

____ a. All living creatures sleep.

____ b. All people need the same amount of sleep.

____ c. About two of every three people are able to remember their dreams when they wake up.

____ d. It is possible to go without sleep for two days with no ill effects.

____ e. Sleep is a passive state during which the body and mind are completely at rest.

3. Fatigue is not due just to hard work or lack of sleep. Other factors can lead to physical exhaustion.

   Read Luke 10:38–42. Martha had a special reason for working so hard—Jesus was a guest in her home! But why was she so irritable?

   Now look at 1 Kings 19:1–3. Why was Elijah so tired?

   Read Deuteronomy 33:27a for God's message to Martha, Elijah, and you. Why are these words helpful?

4. Fatigue is a natural consequence of work. It signals our body to take time to rest and renew. Fatigue can, however, indicate a problem that a good night's sleep cannot cure.

   Do you find yourself using tiredness as an excuse for not participating in activities that would be good for you and your family? Do you find yourself praying for more energy so you can do more or for forgiveness for not meeting responsibilities? Do you wear your fatigue as a badge of honor, indicating you do far more than should be expected of you and therefore are indispensable to your family, church, or God? What could be at the root of those feelings? Turn to Galatians 5:1 to discover what Christ has done for you.

Our forgiving Savior has set us free from the guilt of "I have to, ought to, need to, got to" and from the stress of "it's up to me" or "I should have." When our service is motivated by and dedicated to Him, its timing and completion are also in His hands.

Power for the Present

1. Just as you would sit down and determine how much money to spend on an item based on how much money you have altogether, calculate your time budget and consider where you spend your time. Indicate about how much time you spend each day on these activities. Write "W" for those activities you delay till the weekend.

Category	Number of Hours per Day
Work at a job	_______
Work at home	_______
Family Activities	_______
Church Activities	_______
Social Activities	_______
Leisure Activities	_______
Eating	_______
Personal Grooming	_______
Sleeping	_______
Exercise	_______
Devotion/Prayer	_______
Other	_______

Did seeing your proportionate use of time surprise you? Did it add up to 24 hours in a day? In what areas do you feel you spend too much time? In which areas would you like to spend more time? What factors help or hinder you in budgeting your time wisely?

2. Let's take a look at Jesus' use of time. Read Mark 6:30–56, which lists the activities of a very busy day. As we see Jesus' feeding of the 5000, His stilling of the storm, and His healing of the people, and also His taking time to rest, we are reminded that Jesus is Lord of all our lists and is the power source for all we do.

   Jesus, as true man, was subject to human needs. Look at the following passages and list strategies Jesus used to renew and refresh Himself for the tasks He faced.

a. Matthew 4:11 ______________________________

b. Matthew 12:15 ______________________________

c. Matthew 14:23 ______________________________

d. Matthew 20:34 ______________________________

e. Matthew 26:6–7 ______________________________

f. Matthew 26:37–39 ______________________________

g. Mark 1:35 ______________________________

h. Mark 3:14 ______________________________

i. Luke 4:16 ______________________________

Put a check by the strategies you have used yourself.

3. Remember that physical health is a gift from God to care for and respect thankfully. What can help you to maintain good health?

What do you like to do to rejuvenate when you feel physically tired?

Pray that with God's help you may be able to do these very things!

Promise for the Future

Have you noticed how often people describe themselves as being "sick and tired"? How is physical health related to fatigue? Is it also possible to be "sick and tired" spiritually? There are three ways of dealing with tiredness. The first has to do with prevention: How can you fortify yourself so you are strong enough to deal with the tasks expected of you? The second has to do with emergency "First Aid": What can you do in a crisis, when the breath has been knocked out of you and you can barely function? The third has to do with longevity and endurance: How can you assure a lifetime of commitment and service, avoiding the burnout to which many succumb?

Again, God's Word has answers for us. Divide into three groups. Each group should choose one of the following aspects and study the Bible verses relating to it. Then write out God's "prescription for a healthy physical and spiritual life." Share your findings with the whole group.

℞ *Vitamins for Vitality*
Philippians 4:4–13

℞ *Emergency Treatment*
Isaiah 40:29–31
Isaiah 41:10, 13

℞ *Long-term Therapy*
Colossians 1:9–14
Ephesians 3:16–20

Choose one of the passages we have considered in this study, write it on a piece of paper, and carry it with you to read when you become weary. Better yet, commit it to memory.

Certainty

The prescription for weariness is rest. God made our bodies to require it and practiced it Himself as He rested from His labors after creating the world. As we are at rest, God works. Without our efforts He created the world. Without our efforts Jesus lived and died and rose again for us. Without our efforts the Holy Spirit puts saving faith into our hearts and nourishes it. All that God has accomplished in and for us frees and empowers us to respond with energy, strength, and vitality. When we feel we have had the wind knocked out of us, the Spirit breathes into us new life through His Word and sacraments. When our busyness keeps us from depending on God, He reminds us that He is never too busy for us. He wraps us in His open arms and holds our self-imposed burdens for awhile. We can rest there in safety. When, by the power of the Holy Spirit, we use the strategies Jesus modeled and trust in God's promises to sustain us, we will be renewed and refreshed.

Prayer

Thank God for a body that is able to be renewed through care and rest. Thank Him for loving us when we are at our worst as well as when we are at our best; for loving us when we try to do it all as well as when we neglect to do our share. Ask for His forgiveness for the times we have remained sleepless due to worry or concern. Praise Him for the eternal rest we have been promised through Jesus, our Savior. Then read or sing this stanza of "Come unto Me, Ye Weary" (*LW* 345).

"Come unto me, ye weary, And I will give you rest."
  O blessed voice of Jesus, Which comes to hearts opprest!
It tells of benediction, Of pardon, grace, and peace,
  Of joy that has no ending, Of love that cannot cease.

You and Me, Lord, ...
as I become emotionally drained!

Reflection: Gurgle or Glug?

Have you ever sung this silly camp song?

Alice jumped in the bathtub
To soak away the strain.
She pulled out the plug,
And glug, glug, glug,
She was washed right down the drain.

Do you ever feel like poor Alice—caught in the whirlpool of forces beyond your control until you are consumed and there is nothing left?

God, through the words of the psalmist, offers renewal to those who feel drained. Join now in reading this portion of the psalm together.

Psalm 56—A Paraphrase

O God, I have tried incessantly to transmit Your love to people about me. ...

But I feel as if I had been used, O God.

People have wiped their feet on me.

They take what I offer and then go their way totally oblivious to my problems and pains. ...

But even as I groan in complaint, O Lord, I know that this is Your course for me.

Even as they use You, so they will use me.

Truly, O God, I have nothing to lose,

For it is in losing that I truly find that which is of everlasting value.

You are aware of my frustrations, my feelings of emptiness and loneliness.

You have promised to replenish my vessel, to make me a channel for Your eternal springs. ...

I must be emptied again and again—

Only to be filled from Your boundless resources and then to pour out once more Your blessings upon those in need.

From *Psalms/Now,* by Leslie Brandt. ©1973 CPH.

Pardon for the Past

1. It sometimes feels like everyone makes demands of us—of our time, our attention, our emotions. You are deluged by outside pressures and expectations. Your work commands commitment. Family and friends have needs only you seem equipped to meet. The telephone uncannily knows to ring the second you pour a cup of coffee and sit down with the newspaper. You are not imagining it. God has put you right smack in the middle of people who depend on you.

   Ask yourself, where are you spending your energy? In the cluster chart below, list the names of people or pressures that require your time and attention. Branch out from those words to expand the clusters, if you desire. You may also draw lines to attach interrelationships among the branches.

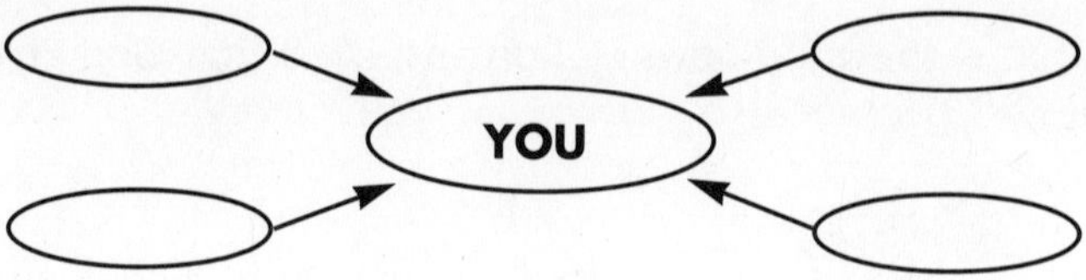

2. It gets complicated, doesn't it? No wonder you feel depleted. As you think about all these demands on your time, emotions, and energy, where on the following scale are your feelings right now?

3. Because you are a child of God and He has created you with feelings of care, concern, and responsibility, you are likely to experience all of the preceding emotions at some time or another as you deal with life on a day-to-day basis. We know how we should feel, but sometimes, like in the psalm we read earlier, we just feel used up.

   Picture yourself as God intended you, a person full of all the God-given gifts and characteristics which make you competent and complete. Then look at what you are today, and you will see that something is wrong with this picture: there are *holes* and *leaks* that are emotionally draining. Read the following verses from Scripture to identify some of the *holes* and *leaks* people have in their lives.

a. Psalm 73:3 ______________________________

b. Ephesians 4:26 ___________________________

c. Philippians 2:3 ___________________________

d. Proverbs 28:25 ___________________________

e. Matthew 18:32–34 _________________________

f. Luke 6:37 ________________________________

g. Romans 7:18–19 __________________________

4. All of these flaws could be summarized by one word: sin. Because sin is a part of our very nature and because we live in a sinful world, we are susceptible to its effects. We are especially susceptible to feelings of guilt when we compare what we are with what we think we "should be." If we try to rely on our own resources to deal with this, what are we like? (See Jeremiah 2:13.)

5. What is the good news in Romans 4:7–8 that God gives to us "leaky" people?

God does not leave us to drain away with a glug, glug, glug. By His death for us on the cross, Jesus has "plugged our leaks," forgiving the sinfulness which destroys and weakens us. Through faith strengthened by the Holy Spirit working through God's Word, we remain connected to His pipeline of forgiveness.

Power for the Present

1. Praise God that He has forgiven our failures and weaknesses; but how do we go on from here when we feel so empty, as if there is not a drop of emotional strength left? God has solved that problem too. To what is His love and mercy compared in Psalm 36:9?

That gurgling sound you hear is the ever-flowing fountain of God's grace. A fountain is a continually bubbling source of replenishment. Just as natural springs well up from deep within the earth to provide refreshing, constantly flowing waters, so God's empowering love in Christ continues to flow freely to refresh and revive us.

2. Jesus calls us to Himself, for He is the source of living water. Read John 4:10–14 and 7:37–38. Analyze this living water. What is its purpose and permanence?

3. God not only pours out His forgiveness on us, He also pours on us the renewing and refreshing power of the Holy Spirit. Feeling drained? Rely on the resources—the means of His grace—supplied by God Himself. God's supply is never depleted. What promise do we find in Philippians 4:19?

4. Use the cluster chart below as a reminder of God's action in your life. Put your name in the center and indicate all the blessings He provides to you, in the name of our Savior Jesus Christ.

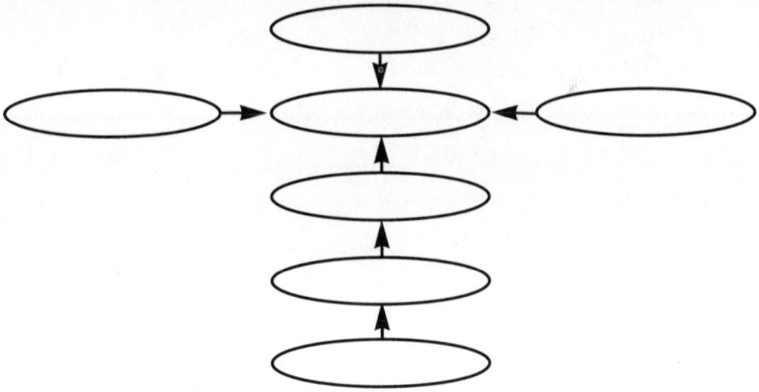

Promise for the Future

1. In this world, we will continue to experience pressures by outside demands and expectations. There may be times we would wish for instant might or miracles. God can, but doesn't need to work in that way. Read in 1 Kings 19:9–18 about a time that Elijah was emotionally drained. How did God come to him to revive and renew him?

2. God works in us through the means of grace—His Word and sacraments. The more closely connected we are to His Word, the wider is the pipeline for replenishment. Through His Word we learn that we are His forgiven and renewed children. No matter how drained we may feel, the reality is that God fills our cup of salvation full to the brim.

   What gentle whisper from God's Word brings a special blessing of calm, peace, and assurance to you?

3. Now consider these practical resources from God's Word as you meet each new day. Complete the rhyming verses, using clues from the Bible verses.

   As you face each brand new day,
   Take the time to stop and ___________. (1 Thessalonians 5:17)

   When demands seem far too great,
   Ask for helpers—___________. (Acts 6:1–4)

   On the worst do you reflect?
   Evaluate what you ___________. (Philippians 1:20)

   Chaos, loose ends, what a strain!
   Learn, prepare, and also ___________. (2 Timothy 3:14–17)

   Cares and worry are selective.
   Keep all things in God's ___________. (2 Corinthians 4:16–18)

   When on the surface you would hide,
   Just summon strength God put ________. (Galatians 5:22–23)

   You can't always be your best
   Without the use of God's gift—___________. (Psalm 127:2)

   Though even in the midst of trial,
   God's gift of humor helps you ___________. (Philippians 4:4)

4. God's people can truly be people of joy. Even in the middle of sad and trying circumstances, we can smile as we remember the warmth of God's care and look for evidence that He is at work in even the smallest details of our lives. Describe the "CROSS-eyed" perspective we have by the power and empowering of the Holy Spirit. (See Ephesians 4:32–5:2.)

5. Psalm 40:1–3 celebrates God's uplifting care. Paraphrase these verses to reflect your own response to God's mercies.

   I waited patiently for the Lord; He

   He lifted me

   He put a new song

Certainty

In a world of sin, we often feel emotionally drained. When we depend on ourselves, we realize our resources are limited. But God, in Christ, has supplied us with a fountain of life. He forgives and heals our sinfulness so that we can be vessels of forgiveness and healing among those whose lives we touch. He provides what we need for our own spiritual and emotional health and equips us so that His love and concern wells up in us as a fountain overflowing from us to others.

Prayer

Rejoice in the many blessings God gives you, especially for the fountain of His grace that overflows with His love and forgiveness. Share this benediction:

May the God of hope fill you with all joy and peace as you trust in Him, so that you may *overflow* with hope by the power of the Holy Spirit. Romans 15:13

You and Me, Lord, ...

as I become spiritually challenged!

Reflection: Christ is the Answer. What is the Question?

Do you have your list ready? You know the one I mean—the list of all those questions you plan to ask God when you get to heaven, all the things you've never understood and always wondered about. Some may be biblical: How did Noah take care of all those animals on the ark? Some may be theological: How can one God be three Persons? But most often they are personal: Why do You let Your children experience the ravages of disease? Why do the wicked prosper and the "innocent" suffer? Where were You, God, when my husband left or when I lost my job? Why haven't You answered my prayer yet? Why didn't You answer in the way I wanted? Why?

In order to satisfy our endless and insistent queries, it looks like God will have a lot of explaining to do. But do we, indeed, have the right to challenge Him? Is it not blasphemous for us to question the almighty God?

"Why?" He might say. "Why do you ask? Are you inquisitor or disciple? Do you intend to accuse or to learn? Do you question out of doubt or in the context of faith?"

Join the psalmist in addressing some of these concerns as you ask God to prepare your hearts and minds to seek and accept His answers.

Psalm 42—A Paraphrase

As a desert wanderer longs for springs of cool water, so my thirsty soul reaches out for You, O God.

How I long for a deeper sense of Your presence, for a faith that will embrace You without fear or doubt!...

And while I struggle with the sickness of doubt, people about me say, "If God is not dead, where is He?"
Oh foolish heart, why do you seethe in unrest? God has not changed; His love for me is ever the same.
I must renew my faith in God;
I must again shout His praises even when I don't feel His presence.
For truly He is God,
and He is my Help and my Hope.

Pardon for the Past

1. Questions, questions, questions. Like a persistent child, we tug at God's coat sleeve with our insistent "Why's." He's used to it. He's heard it before. Can't you almost hear Eve whining, "But why can't we eat of that one tree, huh? Don't you trust us?" Or Noah scratching his head in confusion, "You want me to build a what?" Or Abraham and Sarah chuckling, "Nursery furniture?" Or Peter complaining, "On the water? You're not serious, are you?"

   Now consider Jesus. How did Jesus react when He was faced with a seemingly unreasonable situation? To earth? To die? To rise from the dead? For them? Read the following Bible passages and indicate Jesus' response:

   a. Philippians 2:5–8 ________________________________

   ____

   b. Luke 22:42 ________________________________

   ____

   c. John 15:13 ________________________________

   ____

2. But let's be fair. Not all questioning is the result of doubt or lack of faith. Sometimes we question so we may understand. God has created us as rational beings who want to make sense of the forces around us. We become unsettled when principles we have depended upon seem to crumble away.

   People who live in earthquake country say the most frightening aspect of experiencing a trembler is having their base of support, the very ground under their feet, give way. What is left on which to stand? What is left on which to depend?

So it is when God, upon whom we have always relied, seems to be unpredictable. Questions and doubts scream from our conscious and subconscious thoughts: Why? Where? When? How could You?

Sometimes the search is not so much for answers as it is for discernment. Meet three modern-day Christians, like you, who have some serious questions for the Lord.

My name is Diane. I had always thought God would bless me with a happy home. But life didn't happen the way I planned. My husband isn't exactly a Christian. I figured he would change when he got older and everything would turn out fine. But he didn't. Then God blessed us with a wonderful son. He was a strong witness to his dad about his faith in Jesus. But then ... I can still hardly talk about it. There was the terrible call in the middle of the night. An accident. I know God isn't the cause of the pain, but, why did He let it happen?

I'm Carla. I know the Bible says God answers prayers, and that He wants me to be happy. So I pray a lot because I could use a lot of help. I would like to meet and marry a nice caring man. And another thing, I need to find a better job. I want to know God's will for my life so I'll know how to make those kinds of decisions. I'm tired of waiting for real life to start. Where is God right now, when I need Him?

Call me Lilleth, and call me mad. Whatever happened to the calm predictable church I used to attend? Now we never follow the same order of service twice in a row. And how can I praise God when the music is so fast and loud? Where is the God I used to know? Can He still find me now that my usual pew has been removed to make room for the percussion section?

3. Consider the questions these three women raise. What questions have you faced? Do you see fear in any of these questions? Fear of what? What does Psalm 56:8–13 tell us about fear and faith?

As we feel spiritually challenged by the events in our lives, we can be certain that although we may not understand the reasons for what we experience, our God does. If we feel frustrated by the answers we are given, perhaps we are not asking the right questions. We may not know all the *why's*. But we do know *who*.

4. John the Baptist had a question for the Lord. Only one question, but it was a vitally important one. John wanted to know *who.* Read Luke 7:18–23. John was in the process of devoting his life to the Messiah. Now one more time, he needed to know, from Jesus' own lips, are You the One?

   a. To what did Jesus' reassuring reply draw attention?

   b. These observations would have made double sense to John. They were miraculous events in and of themselves. But what other significance did they have? (See Isaiah 35:5–6.)

5. When you come to the Lord with questions, begging for reassurance that He is, indeed, who He claims to be and will do what He promises, to what does He direct your attention? Read Psalm 105:1 and 5. Then consider the blessings He has given in the past that are evidence of His power, credibility, and faithfulness. List some that you have known personally.

6. We know the strength and joy of the Lord, but the devil loves to attempt to steal it. He tempts us to turn our eyes away from Jesus and worry about other matters. Our sinful nature falls easily into his diversionary plans. Guilt convinces us we are unworthy of God's love. Pride insists that we understand and agree with all that happens. Fear binds us in helpless bundles of self-defense. In such a turbulent state of being, we challenge God Himself to make everything right. And He does.

   First, God makes us right with Himself by forgiving the lack of faith which results in our panic and despair. He freed us from guilt by taking away all condemnation through Jesus' death on the cross. Then He clears our heads to remember how He has helped His people throughout history and how He has been with us throughout our own lives.

   Next, He calms our hearts with His powerful Word of comfort and assurance and strengthens us so we are equipped for all situations in which we might find ourselves.

Finally, He rescues us in the way and at the time that is best. As Satan hurls the lightening bolts of adversity our way, God grasps them for His inspection and allows nothing past Him that will be too much for us.

Power for the Present

1. Job, in the Old Testament, is the epitome of one who was spiritually challenged. Observe him as an example of ways in which God provides for us in the midst of trials and doubts. Pretend you are interviewing Job for your local newspaper. What are his answers to these questions?

   a. WHO was the cause of your problems? (Job 2:7)

   ____

   b. WHAT were some of the difficulties you faced? (Job 1:13–19; 2:7)

   ____

   c. WHO tried to give you advice? (Job 2:9, 11)

   ____

   d. WHERE did all your blessings originate? (Job 1:21)

   ____

   e. WHEN will you stop trusting in God? (Job 13:15)

   ____

   f. HOW do you feel about God even now? (Job 19:23–27; 42:2–3)

   ____

   Epilog. How did God respond to Job's troubles? God reminded Job that He is the Lord. He does not need to explain Himself. But His care never stopped. He restored all Job had lost and more.

2. As always, Jesus provides the best example. He too was spiritually challenged by the "Master of Doubts"—Satan himself. Read Matthew 4:1–11. Consider the devil's timing and strategies. Then see where Jesus summoned strength with which to face Satan's attacks.

a. Jesus turned for power to the Word of God. When Satan tried to misdirect His focus by misquoting Scripture, Jesus combated with what He knew to be true. In what ways do you or can you have God's Word as a readily available resource for your times of doubt or trouble?

b. Another source of strength, prayer, is alluded to in verse 2. (Fasting in Scripture is generally associated with prayer, as a person focused all his attention on spiritual rather than physical concerns.) We see Jesus relying on prayer often in His ministry (Luke 5:16). Choose one of these verses and explain why it brings comfort to you: Psalm 139:1–3; Romans 8:26; Isaiah 65:24.

c. Notice the follow-up of Jesus' encounter (Matthew 4:11). After our battles, when we are bruised and exhausted, God continues to provide loving support. What promise does He offer in Hebrews 1:14?

d. Soon after His confrontation with Satan, Jesus enlisted another source of help. Identify it in Matthew 4:18–22. Christian friends can be a powerful source of strength. Who among your acquaintances can provide that support? With whom can you pray and seek God's will? If you do not have a close brother or sister in Christ, pray for one now. What other steps could you follow to identify and form such a friendship?

3. Consider this: Where was God during the highs and lows you have experienced in your life? Was He above you to challenge you? Below you to support you? Was He always near? What do these verses tell you about God's presence?

a. Deuteronomy 32:9–11 ______________________________

b. Psalm 139:9–10 ______________________________

c. Isaiah 43:1–2 ______________________________

Promise for the Future

Have you ever watched an artisan weave a tapestry or rug? Threads are placed on a loom in two different directions. Some extend up and down (the warp). Others are woven in and out from side-to-side (the woof). Until the entire tapestry is finished the design makes no sense. There are loose ends and knots and rather ugly patterns which emerge. But the weaver continues weaving, and we observers have confidence that the creator of the work knows what he is doing.

When the project is complete, we can step back and appreciate the total picture. We still may not understand every step along the way, but the finished product is just as the weaver intended from the beginning—a thing of beauty.

So it is with our lives. The vertical threads in the tapestry represent God's dealings with us. Interspersed throughout our years are the horizontal relationships we have with other people. We may not know at any given time why one color is used and not another or why a strand is cut or knotted. But we know who the Creator is. We know He is developing us for use in His kingdom and equipping us for His service.

Some day, when we view our lives from the "right" side of heaven, we may appreciate the designs and nuances which God included. Then we will be off the loom and into the room of the mansion which He has prepared. Until then He invites us to look at life through His eyes—trusting His power and faithfulness.

Certainty

As human beings, we often do not understand the turns our lives take. We are tempted to trust in our own judgment and doubt God's power and intentions. Through Jesus, our Savior, who became a human being and was tempted as we are, God forgives our unbelief. He assures us that in spite of the apparent evidence of the present moment, He will work all things together for the good of those who love Him. We can trust Him for all things in this life and the next.

Prayer

Pray with the frenzied father in Mark 9:24, "I do believe; help me overcome my unbelief!" Read together the reassurance of Romans 8:38–39.

You and Me, Lord, ...

as I seek new opportunities to serve You!

Reflection: No Strings Attached

Did you hear about Samantha Jones? She really got herself tied up in knots. First she got involved in the membership class; then she got involved in LWML; then she got involved in the women's choir; then she got involved in the altar guild; then she got involved in teaching Sunday school; then she got involved in the "Sunshine Committee"; then she got involved in the health and fitness ministry; finally she involved herself right out of the church!

Does that sound too close to home? There are so many opportunities for service in the church and in our world, how do we know where to start—or when to stop?

Turn your hearts and minds toward God's involvement in your life as you read this psalm responsively.

Psalm 40 — A Paraphrase

I searched long and shouted loud for God ...
and He responded.
He reached into my pathetic emptiness
and planted objective and purpose there.
Now I feel like singing;
there is genuine meaning for my life. ...
Our God is not looking for genius; He does not require great talents.
He is not charmed by our panic-ridden activity.
He simply asks for our faith and our obedience.
It was when I turned from self-seeking to embrace His will for my life that I discovered serenity and security.

Thus I am compelled to express in word and in deed the glad news of God's love and concern to anyone who will listen. ...

I still feel overwhelmed at times by my faults and [failures]. ...

I need to rely continuously on the grace of God.

God grant that all who search for life's meaning

May discover such in a relationship of love and trust in Him. ...

As for me, foolish and sinful though I am, I know that God will never cease to love me. Amen.

From *Psalms/Now,* by Leslie Brandt. ©1973 CPH.

Pardon for the Past

1. On the lines below list projects to which you are now committed that involve service to the church, your family, or others. Think in terms of committees, organizations, special tasks, and the like.

   Now, in front of each commitment put a plus sign by those which make you feel genuinely happy and which you look forward to doing; put a check mark by those which you do willingly, but with reservation; put a minus sign by those which you do not enjoy but take part in because you have to or because you would feel guilty if you didn't.

   Are you caught up in a tangle of shoulds and musts? What keeps you doing those things you don't really like? What keeps you from doing what you really would like?

2. On the basis of your list, which of the following best describe your involvement?

can't

challenged by **interested in**

enjoying it **willing to** **responsible for**

have to **expected to** **don't want to**

won't

Are any of these responses more "right" or "wrong" than the others? We would probably make such an analysis according to the details of the situation, personalities and abilities involved, and time available. How does God look at things (1 Samuel 16:7)?

God looks at the motivation. *Why* we do what we do is far more important to Him than *what* we do.

3. When we serve others because we feel we must or because we would feel guilty if we didn't or because we want to get something in return, we are living under the Law. The *shoulda, oughta, haveta, gotta syndrome* takes the joy out of serving others. Identify the feelings living under the Law evokes in the following examples.

John joined the Parent Teacher League when his son, Robby, was in kindergarten. He wanted to be involved in his son's education. He was determined he would not fail to meet his responsibilities. After facing an hour of bumper-to-bumper traffic on the highway, he didn't even have time to go home to eat dinner. But he made it to the monthly meeting; he had to be there to watch out for Robby's welfare. He was so tired when he finally got home, he didn't have much patience left for Robby's silly games or to read him a story. Being a responsible parent is serious business.

Shannon was often too busy to phone her mother to chat. When the call came that her mother had died, she thought her heart would break. Now she tries to make up for it. She spends every Tuesday and Thursday night doing volunteer work at the retirement home. The night her husband surprised her with concert tickets she felt really bad about not going with him. But she wouldn't let those poor elderly people down just for the sake of her own pleasure. Shannon was not going to make that mistake again—she would always have time for others.

When was the last time Rosie had a moment to herself? The phone rang just as she was tossing some spaghetti in the pot for her family to eat for dinner. It was Edith asking her to be a substitute teacher on Sunday so she could get away for the weekend. Edith pleaded with Rosie to not let her down. Rosie grudgingly agreed. Teaching was not something she did well, but someone had to do it. She wished she had time to join the church choir; now that's something she would like to do. But it seemed like she was always picking up the pieces for Edith. (The water on the stove wasn't the only thing boiling in the kitchen.)

4. Those feelings were not what God had in mind when He called us to commitment. Read Romans 7:5–6. What are two possible motivations for our actions?

5. We are either driven by the Law or empowered by the Spirit. How can you tell which is which? The answer lies in who is in control. As long as we are bound by our sinful nature, Satan jerks our strings like a sadistic puppeteer, delighting in our discomfort and confusion. He laughs in glee because he knows all that energy and motion is worthless. Any efforts aroused by the Law leave us dangling in sin because we are powerless on our own.

   BUT, God has cut the cords with His cross-shaped shears and released us to serve Him as His living children—no strings attached. We act, now, enabled by the Holy Spirit, who directs us from within. We have been set free by the cross of Christ and are empowered for what purpose (Galatians 5:13)?

6. Another factor to consider is WHOM we are serving. When your efforts leave you feeling inept or unappreciated, or when people frustrate or disappoint, what encouragement can you find in these Scripture verses? Hebrews 9:14; Matthew 25:40; 1 Corinthians 10:31; Romans 12:1, 11.

Power for the Present

1. Let's take a close look at some faithful servants described in Scripture who served in the "new way of the Spirit" which Paul described. As individuals or as a small group read the verses and consider
   - *who* served and was served;
   - *what* type of service was given;
   - *how* God prepared that person for service; and
   - *why* the person became involved in serving.

a. Ruth 1:15–19; 2:2–3; 4:13–17

b. 1 Samuel 1:1–2:21

c. Acts 9:36–42

d. Acts 16:13–15

e. Acts 18:1–3, 24–26; Romans 16:3–4

f. Now consider a person you know personally who serves God and His people. Identify the same components.

Praise God for the way He works in our lives and through others!

2. When faced with an opportunity to serve, many people assume a serious and worried look, clasp their hands together tightly, and ponder deeply:

What is God's will regarding this decision? If I do it, will He be pleased? If I don't do it, will He be angry? What if I do it and decide later I shouldn't have, or don't do it and decide later I should? Is it right? Is it wrong? Is it possible? I guess I will. No, I won't. Yes—No—I just don't know. Dear God, why don't You show me what I should do?

By this time it is late in the night—your pillow is pocked with headprints. Your stomach is in a knot, your head aches, and your joy is nowhere to be found.

Guess what! If you decline, the Lord will get the job done another way. If you say yes, He will provide the resources you need. Your answer is not what is most important. Your attitude of faith and commitment to Him is. And even that faith is His doing. Yes or no, you are still His child. Yes or no, His will is done; that's His responsibility—not yours. Yes or no, you have the assurance of forgiveness and renewal because God has already said yes to you. What profound blessings does Jesus give to us, His people in faith? See John 14:26–27 and John 17:13, 26.

Promise for the Future

1. In Isaiah 42:1 the prophet calls the Messiah a servant. Jesus said of Himself, "The Son of Man did not come to be served, but to serve" (Matthew 20:28). Picture Jesus, the Suffering Servant, giving His all for you. Read about the loving acts Jesus performed for you in Philippians 2:1–11.

   In these verses, Scripture also challenges you, one who has been served, to "let your attitude be the same." Namely, be as committed to and excited about service as Jesus was, humbly and gratefully expressing your love in return. God can use your lips and hands and legs and heart for His good purposes.

   God can work through many means. He used a ________ to help bring His message to Balaam (Numbers 22:21–35). He used a ________ to display His priceless Gift, born as a human child (Luke 2:7). He was ready to audition __________ to sing in His choir (Luke 19:37–40). He will use anyone and anything that serves His purposes—even you and me!
2. Can you identify some ways God has prepared and equipped you for His service? In Column A, list some of your interests and talents. In Column B, list experiences you have had through which God taught you something that could be of value to others. In Column C, list people God has brought within your sphere of influence or knowledge who have needs you could address.

A	B	C

3. Do your lists indicate a direction or focus for new areas of service? Where might God be leading you? Write a prayer thanking God for His gifts and asking Him to guide, motivate, and equip you to lovingly and joyfully serve Him as He sees fit.

Certainty

Christ frees us from the bonds of sin and guilt to serve Him with joy. He empowers and equips us for His work and graciously blesses our efforts, using us to demonstrate His love in the world. As His gift of salvation is free from all constraint, we serve Him gladly, without fear or guilt—no strings attached!

Prayer

Our service to God and others is a response of joy. Psalm 100:2 RSV says, "Serve the LORD with gladness!" Choose several verses from this list to read aloud about our joy in the Lord: Psalm 16:11, 28:7, 47:1, 67:4, 71:23, 90:14, 92:4, 94:19, 95:1, 98:4, 126:2.

You and Me, Lord, ...

as I celebrate relationships blessed by You!

Reflection: You and Us Together, Lord

Do you know the secret for getting a blackened, crusty casserole dish really clean? Simply bake something in it and take it to a friend. It's guaranteed she will return it spotless, better than it was before! You would do the same for her, right? That's what friends are for. The nail-mangling, knuckle-skinning scrubbing you wouldn't do for yourself, you do willingly for someone you love.

God created us as social beings. Our relationship with each other is based on our relationship with Him. "Dear friends, let us love one another, for love comes from God" (1 John 4:7). Join in celebrating God's gift of fellowship as you pray this psalm responsively.

Psalm 133 and 134 — A Paraphrase

O God, how precious it is for us and how pleasing it must be to You when Your [children] and servants learn how to live and work together in unity!

It is in the measure that we do this that we begin to resemble You and to carry out most effectively Your purposes in our disjointed and discordant world.

Come, let us together bless His name,

rejoice in His loving concern for us,

Declare His worth to all creatures,

and walk in obedience to His will.

It is the same God who made heaven and earth and all of us who dwell therein.

Let us worship and serve Him together. Amen.

From *Psalms/Now,* by Leslie Brandt. © 1973 CPH.

Pardon for the Past

1. Use the acrostic below to define some characteristics of a friend. (The letters can come anywhere in the words you write—at the beginning, middle, or end.)

F

R

I

E

N

D

Do you have a friend who matches this description? Are *you* a friend who matches this description?

2. Divide into small groups. Each person may choose one sentence starter and complete the thought. (Choose any one you wish, even if others have chosen the same one.)

a. My best friend and I like …

b. I'll never forget the time a friend …

c. Once I had a troubled friendship …

d. My friend and I had so much fun when …

e. I was so frightened (sad) when my friend …

f. One of my friends is a real blessing to me because …

To summarize what you have been discussing, complete this statement: When it comes to friends, ______________________

____

3. The preschool class sat on the floor, listening to a story. Kurt and Carlos couldn't leave each other alone. Kurt poked Carlos with his elbow; Carlos poked Kurt in return. The tussling went on until the teacher finally suggested, "Boys, you are causing so much trouble for each other. Why don't you sit on opposite sides of the room so you won't be bothered?" Kurt's mouth dropped open and his eyes stared incredulously. "But," he explained, "we're friends!"

Even friends sometimes get on each other's nerves. Even friends have their limits. Even friends, perhaps *especially* friends, can hurt each other.

Take a look at the motley crew who called themselves friends of Jesus—His 12 disciples. Can you guess the identities of these better-known members of the group?

a. I can out-fish, out-boast, and out-preach anyone. I'm fearless—to a point. When I was called on to stand up for my Friend, I denied Him instead. _________ (Mark 14:66–68)

b. I am a person of unquestioned loyalty. I believed everything Jesus ever told me—well, except for that one time I had to see and feel for myself before I was really convinced. _________ (John 20:24–25)

c. We were always Jesus' favorites. We knew if He liked us best He would give us places of honor in His kingdom. We really felt bad about falling asleep that time when He asked us to support Him in prayer. ______ and ______. (Mark 10:35–37)

d. I liked Jesus, I really did. He asked me to be His disciple, didn't He? He even greeted me with a kiss and trusted me with the money. I didn't expect things would turn out the way they did. _________ (Matthew 26:47–50)

Denial, doubt, greed, betrayal. Were those some of the attributes you listed to describe a friend? Have you ever been guilty of the same behavior and attitudes in your relationships with other people—or with God?

4. Sin taints every relationship—even those God intended to be wonderful—because every earthly relationship is made up of human beings who are sinners. When sin destroyed the relationship between God and man, it also destroyed the relationship between people.

What was Adam's first response when God asked why he was hiding? Did he defend his wife, and did they stand together for support? No, he pointed his juice-stained finger in her direction and said, "She made me do it—the woman *You* gave me is to blame." (See Genesis 3:12.)

Cain and Abel followed in their parents' footsteps. Brotherhood had its beginning, but jealousy prevailed. Fellowship disintegrated into hate, and resulted in death—the ultimate separation. (See Genesis 4:3–8.)

Have you seen relationships turn sour? Do you know people who will not speak to each other or work together or forgive one another? Such alienation is heartbreaking. It broke God's heart too. He couldn't stand to see His own people separated from Himself. What did God do to change this situation? See Colossians 1:21–22; 2 Corinthians 5:18–21.

Are there people that *you* do not speak to or work with or forgive? Then remember you have a Friend in Christ Jesus, who wants to reconcile you to each other just as He has already reconciled you to Himself.

Power for the Present

1. When children gather to play ball, the ritual usually begins by choosing up sides. You know the routine. Everyone lines up along the fence while the two captains call out names. Good athletes are the first to be chosen. Then the rest of the names are called, until the last poor soul is left, his lack of prowess evident to all ... UNLESS ..., unless the poorest player is a friend of the captain. Then that person is assured of being chosen early in the bidding—not on the basis of skill, but on the basis of friendship, which covers a multitude of errors.

   What a picture that process is of our placement on Jesus' team! Jesus has chosen you! Read John 15:15–17.

   a. On what basis did Jesus choose us? Did it have anything to do with our own worth?

   b. Out of His great and undeserved love, God decided from all eternity that we should be His friends. He accomplished this through Jesus' death for us on the cross. Jesus points out that He did not call us to be merely servants, but to be friends. What is the difference?

   c. Now that we are His friends, what does He ask us to do?

2. The Bible contains many examples of friendship. Perhaps the most compelling is the story of two unlikely cohorts—David and Jonathan. Read about the covenant between the two friends in 1 Samuel 18:1–4 and 20:42.

A covenant is a promise—a binding commitment between two parties—somewhat like a contract. A "unilateral" covenant is one that depends on only one of the people involved. It is instigated by him and carried out by him, regardless of what the second person says or does. (If you promise your child $5.00 per week allowance, you have made a unilateral agreement.)

A "bilateral" covenant is a reciprocal agreement between two parties. It is based on both persons following through on the conditions that are established. (If you pay your child $5.00 for raking leaves, you have made a bilateral agreement.)

a. What kind of covenant did David and Jonathan make?

b. What do you think was significant about the gifts Jonathan gave as a token of the agreement?

c. How did Jonathan carry out his part of the friendship covenant? (1 Samuel 19:1–6)

d. How did David carry out his part of the friendship covenant? (2 Samuel 9:1–7)

e. Read Hebrews 8:6–13. Describe the covenant God has made with us, His people in Christ Jesus—our dearest Friend.

3. God has given people to each other for care, support, and assistance in carrying out His will in the world. Friendship is a relationship that God blesses, and it can occur in many contexts. Some of these relationships are listed on the next page. Add any others that come to mind.

_____ Spouse
_____ Sibling
_____ Friend
_____ Co-worker
_____ Neighbor
_____ Church member
_____ Business person/consumer
_____ Other:_____________
_____ Parent/Child
_____ Extended Family
_____ Employer/Employee
_____ Teacher/Student
_____ Fellow-citizen
_____ Pastor/layperson
_____ Humankind
_____ Other:_____________

a. Rate these relationships, starting with a "1" by the one that is the most important to you. Comment on these questions: Why did you choose as you did? What made the choice difficult? Although we may give some relationships a higher priority than others, what do they all have in common?

b. Choose one from among the relationships listed above and write a word of Scripture or a prayer for this person.

c. What special gift can you bring to a relationship with a person who is not a Christian?

d. What is unique about a relationship that *does* have Christ in common? (Look again at the friendship of Jonathan in 1 Samuel 23:16.)

Promise for the Future

God has an action plan for us to develop and strengthen our relationships. Choose one of these portions of Scripture to read, and then list traits the Holy Spirit desires to nurture in your life: Ephesians 4:32–5:2; Colossians 3:12–17; Acts 2:42–47; Philippians 4:4–8; James 3:17–18.

Certainty

God has established a relationship between us and Himself by reconciling us through the death of Jesus, our Savior. He has also given us other people for mutual care and support. As He has forgiven us, He empowers us to live in love and forgiveness with each other. He blesses these relationships and invites us to join together with each other to serve and praise Him.

Prayer

Celebrate relationships that have developed in your group by thanking God in prayer for one another. Share the bond of blessing that Jonathan spoke to David (1 Samuel 20:42): *The Lord shall be between you and me!* Join hands and sing or pray together this hymn (*LW* 295).

Blest be the tie that binds
  Our hearts in Christian love.
The unity of heart and mind
  Is like to that above.

Before our Father's throne
  We pour our ardent prayers;
Our fears, our hopes, our aims are one,
  Our comforts and our cares.

Leaders Notes

You and Me, Lord, ...
as I experience brokenness caused by sin!

Reflection: "Fix It, Please!"

Begin by reading the introductory paragraphs. Lead into a responsive reading of the psalm.

Pardon for the Past

1. After reading the introductory paragraph aloud, use the opening activity as a discussion starter.

2. Depending on the size and nature of your group, do the suggested activity individually, in small groups, or as a class. Emphasize the fact that brokenness causes pain and sorrow.

d. Genesis 27 is an example of a family broken by deceit and jealousy.

a. Luke 22 shows how Peter is devastated by his broken promise of faithfulness.

e. 2 Samuel 11 is the story of both David and Bathsheba breaking marriage vows.

f. 2 Samuel 18 depicts David's heart-broken grief at the death of his son.

b. Genesis 37 portrays Joseph's idealistic dream, which later seems to be shattered as he is sold into slavery.

c. Genesis 3 takes us back to the beginning of it all—the basic break in the relationship between God and man.

3. The cause of this brokenness is sin. Read the summary paragraphs aloud. You might reflect with your class what the world would be like if sin had not entered the picture. We can only conjecture. But imagine the intensity of Adam and Eve's emotions and sense of loss after having had a taste of the world God had in mind. The knowledge of good and evil which they had desired made it clear that they were guilty. They didn't even think to ask God for a second chance. God, however, thought of it Himself and immediately set His redemptive plan in motion.

Power for the Present

1. The strand of God's love for His people could not be broken. The picture of the serpent/seed was a vivid one, fully understood by Adam and Eve. When Cain was born (according to Martin Luther's translation of Genesis 4:1) Eve exclaimed, "I have the man, the Lord." She was hoping for a quick fix. Little did she know how long the world would wait for the Savior to come and win the ultimate victory.

2. At the right and chosen time, Jesus came to reconcile our relationship with God through His death and resurrection, offering the certainty that nothing can ever separate us from His love.

3. This set of examples points out that God uses broken people to carry out His will. Again, discuss as many as time permits individually, as a class, or in groups.

* Moses used the excuse that he was a poor speaker. Yet God provided all the resources he needed to convince Pharaoh. Later God spoke with him "face to face" as with a friend—a truly unique relationship established by God.
* Samson was brash and immoral throughout his lifetime. At the end he was physically blinded as well. Yet God used him to defeat His enemies. Samson is listed as one of God's faithful people in Hebrews 11. Only God's grace could use Samson's brokenness as strength.
* Rahab was a prostitute; yet God used her to save the lives of His people. She was an ancestor of David and Jesus; and she too is listed in Hebrews 11.
* God took Hannah from the depths of depression over her childlessness to the joy of becoming the mother of one of Israel's greatest prophets.
* God used the blind man mentioned in John 9 to proclaim to anyone who would listen how Jesus had healed him. His blindness and its cure served the purpose of glorifying God.
* God transformed Paul from a persecutor of Christians into an apostle and missionary. Throughout his life Paul struggled with his sinful nature, just as we deal with ours. But he also knew it was God who had given him the victory through Jesus Christ.
* If the members of the class feel comfortable doing so, ask them to share times when God has been with them in times of brokenness and brought good out of seemingly hopeless situations.

4. The tools that God uses to repair the brokenness in our lives are: (a) prayer, relying on God's promises; (b) God's Word, to show us the way to salvation and His will for our lives; (c) the Lord's Supper, through which God provides forgiveness to each of us in a per-

sonal way; (d) Christian friends, for support and encouragement; (e) forgiveness, as God grants it to us, and as He moves us to deal with others in the same way; (f) trust, that knows God's loving care, which will, along with our salvation through Christ, give us everything we really need; (g) Baptism, as we daily remember the blessings given in this sacrament and rejoice in the assurance that we are children of God.

5. Discuss the multiple choice section as a group. The answers are meant to evoke a variety of responses. *Prayer* provides us the opportunity to communicate with God as we pour out our needs and praise to God. He invites us to pray constantly and considers every request important. *Scripture* is God's Word to us, and it is a means of grace. It is more than interesting stories or a self help book. *The sacrament of the Lord's Supper* is for sinners. Many people worry about their worthiness to receive the Lord's Supper. Jesus made us worthy through faith in His sacrificial death. Regardless of how we look or feel, the power is in our Savior and His words, "Given and shed for you for the remission of sins." *Our Christian friends* may sometimes disappoint us, but we are God's gifts to each other, to encourage and build each other up in the Lord. *Forgiveness* is God's gift offered unconditionally. God calls us to do the same, forgiving others as we have been forgiven—fully and freely. *Trust* ultimately means letting go of our reliance upon anything except God. *Baptism* is not mere tradition; there is power in Baptism—through water and the Word, God gives forgiveness and new life in Christ, blessings in which we daily rejoice. *All these resources are effective through God's power and available to all God's people.*

Promise for the Future

1. Class members may wish to share their thoughts or they may choose to reflect silently on the questions.

2. Discuss the checklist. Consider why it is easier to help some people than others. As human beings with varying backgrounds and experiences we often differentiate in our attitudes and actions. But God cares for us all the same. Even those who do not deserve His love (and that includes us all) receive it fully and freely. Assure participants that Jesus offers complete forgiveness to us when we fail to demonstrate His love to others or harbor a negative attitude toward someone who needs to hear of Jesus' love for them. As His Spirit works in our hearts through the Word, He increases our faith and moves us to be more like Him.

3. Read Ephesians 2:13–22 and celebrate together the future God has in store for us.

4. Close with comments on the fact that being broken leads us to Jesus for help. We have His assurance that He welcomes us each time we come and that He will never withdraw His love from us.

Certainty

You may suggest that group members highlight this section of their books, which summarizes the main thought of the lesson.

Prayer

Suggest that partners or threesomes pray together a prayer thanking God for the healing and wholeness He supplies, or let each person pray silently. Then conclude by praying or singing the hymn stanza together.

SESSION 2

You and Me, Lord, ...

as I become physically tired!

Reflection: Catching Your Second Wind

Read the introductory paragraphs. Then pray the psalm responsively.

Pardon for the Past

1. The inventions of electricity and "labor-saving" machines have been mixed blessings. Now there seems to be no limit to the amount of work that is possible. Discuss how our standards have been stretched to accommodate these possibilities. Numbering the activities should illustrate that people vary in their tolerance for physical and mental tasks. Individual time clocks (morning person/night person) and the motivation for doing certain jobs, as well as their perceived value, all play a part in our feelings about doing them.

2. Most people will know their own body's signals that fatigue is taking over. Possible indications of tiredness could be irritability, forgetfulness, or clumsiness. These reactions undoubtedly affect not only the person experiencing them, but also others with whom they come into contact.

The answers to the "Sleep Quiz" are as follows:

a. False. All vertebrates (animals with backbones) seem to sleep in some form, and many appear to dream. Invertebrates (insects, crustaceans, etc.) have periods of rest from activity, but no brain changes that would indicate sleep.

b. False. Children generally require more sleep than adults. Most people require seven hours or more. People need more sleep during times of stress, change, or new learning.

c. True. Dreams seem to be a way of clearing the mind of unnecessary information. Dreaming may be especially important for learning, reasoning, and emotional adjustment.

d False. Sleep deprivation has serious consequences. After two days without sleep people find that lengthy concentration becomes difficult, they are easily distracted, and are more likely to make mistakes. Longer periods without sleep may result in difficulty seeing and hearing, and in periods of hallucinations and confusion.

e. False. Brain cells are active during sleep. Three fourths of our sleep time is called synchronized sleep, characterized by slow brain waves, regular pulse and breathing, and the absence of rapid eye movements. During this type of sleep people are *physically* renewed. The other portion of our sleep time, desynchronized sleep, is characterized by rapid eye movements and dreaming. During this period of sleep people are *mentally* restored.

3. Martha may have been physically tired, but her attitude toward her sister added to her irritableness. Elijah was emotionally stressed as well as being physically weary. Deuteronomy 33:27a reminds us that we are supported in all our doings by God's strong and unfailing arms. We can be frail; it is His strength that counts. We can rest; He is our support.

4. The questions of warning that are posed indicate that fatigue can be a symptom of misplaced motives. God, in Christ, forgives our sins and leads us to new life. Whatever we do in response to God's love for us in Christ is accepted fully by Him. We do not need to make excuses. And we do not need to assume responsibility for what He can accomplish in His time and according to His will.

Power for the Present

1. The time budget activity illustrates the need for balance in our perspective and in our lives.

2. The example of Jesus' day in Mark 6:30–56 shows that both Jesus and His disciples needed rest. He did help those who needed Him, and He also found time for renewal. Just as God miraculously supplied the food and healing necessary for His people, so He has the power to supply rest and refreshment. We can trust Him to provide what is needed according to His timing.

As you examine Jesus' strategies for renewal, you may want to divide the Bible verses among several groups. Strategies: (a) God sends angels as His messengers of help. (b) Withdraw from threatening circumstances if possible. Choose your battles. (c) Find a pleasant retreat spot for time in prayer. (d) Know the joyful attitude of compassion, responding in willingness to help. (e) Enjoy the hospitality of others. And thankfully appreciate the positive reinforcements you receive when served by others. (f) Surrounded by friends, pray again. (g) Make time to spend with God in solitude and meditation. (h) Delegate responsibility. Don't try to do everything yourself. (i) Worship regularly. Study God's Word.

3. Personal strategies for health and energizing may include exercise, a healthy diet, good medical care, music, art, hobbies, reading, peace and quiet, a simple break in routine, etc.

Promise for the Future

As you consider God's answers for spiritual and physical health, you may want to post three large sheets of paper on which each group's responses can be listed.

Vitamins for Vitality. Have a joyful heart. Avoid worry. Pray. Fill your mind with positive things. Let God's peace guard your heart. Practice contentment. Avoid complaining. Obtain strength from God.

Emergency Treatment. Receive power from God, His form of CPR when feeling faint. Give God your fear. Depend on Him for superhuman strength and power when yours fails. He is right beside you.

Long-term Therapy. As God's child, forgiven in Christ, empowered by the Spirit, live in service, thankfulness, and joy, growing in faith through the power of the Spirit as you continue to study God's Word. Live knowing that Christ *dwells* in you—not just temporarily, but always. You are not just scattered on the surface of the ground of faith; you are deeply rooted in faith by your Baptism and God's continuing love for you. His claim on you does not expire. His resources are available beyond anything you could ever demand or require.

Certainty

Reassure the members of your group that God has made you who you are. If you are a morning person, use that early energy in service to God. If you get your second wind late in the day, don't apologize for not being a morning person. Be yourself as God intended you. Let your work be an act of worship, not a sentence of drudgery. And always rest ... in the Lord.

Prayer

Follow the suggestions indicated.

SESSION 3

You and Me, Lord, ...

as I become emotionally drained!

Reflection: Gurgle or Glug?

Read the introductory paragraphs. Then pray the psalm responsively.

Pardon for the Past

1. Lead the class in the exercise of identifying people and commitments which make demands on their time.

2. As participants identify their feelings on the continuum, point out that there is not a right or wrong answer. It merely indicates a state of mind. Recognize that we will feel tired or even resentful at

times. We have human limitations. But God helps us deal with these negative feelings, forgives any sinfulness involved, and frees us from the guilt that incapacitates our lives.

3. As you read the sections of Scripture as a class or in small groups, discuss some of the ways our resources are depleted.

a. Envy. Not only is it hard to continue positive interaction with someone when we are inwardly jealous of them, we are also left with the unhappiness of discontent.

b. Anger. God desires that we resolve and dissolve our anger because it destroys relationships and our personal joy.

c. Selfish ambition and vain conceit. Focusing only on one's self limits opportunities of service. If self-preservation is our goal, it is impossible to reach out and take emotional risks.

d. Greed. We can't give when our goal is to get.

e. Unmerciful unwillingness to forgive. Carrying a grudge is devastatingly harmful physically, emotionally, and spiritually. Realizing the extent of God's forgiveness to us motivates us also to forgive unconditionally those who have wronged us.

f. Being judgmental. Tearing down others to build yourself up is destructive to all persons involved. In 1 Thessalonians 5:11 we see that God desires that we encourage and build each other up.

g. Unrealistic expectations. When we expect more of people than they are able to give, we become frustrated and angry. This is also true when we expect too much of ourselves. The truth is—we are sinners in a sinful world.

4. As we see our weakness and sin, we see that we are like leaky, broken cisterns (water tanks). We are unable to make the repairs ourselves. We are directed to God for help.

5. The only hope of repair for our broken and sinfilled lives is in Christ and His cross.

Power for the Present

1. Psalm 36:9 compares God's love to a living spring or bubbling fountain.

2. Christ, the fountain of living water, brings eternal life and salvation, which lasts forever.

3. Philippians 4:19 reminds us of the vastness of God's resources, which He makes available to us freely, in Christ.

4. The cluster chart of God's blessings to us demonstrates that He is connected to His people in real and practical ways. His death on the cross linked us to Him forever; He is a part of every aspect of our lives.

Promise for the Future

1. God could have used His power in the wind, earthquake, or fire. But He chose to use a whispering voice to revitalize and reassure Elijah.

2. Have class members share the Bible verses that are especially meaningful to them.

3. Discuss the short poems and Bible verses that suggest approaches for dealing with the days ahead, living in Christ.

... Take the time to stop and *pray*. Our heavenly Father promises to hear and answer according to His good and gracious will.

... Ask for helpers—*delegate*. When the task became too great, the disciples wisely delegated jobs to others who could do them equally well. God gives us each other for support and relief.

... Evaluate what you *expect*. Having realistic expectations relieves frustration and stress.

... Learn, prepare, and also *train*. Preparation and education can help us interact more efficiently and productively. However, we recognize that God's Word is the source of ultimate wisdom.

... Keep all things in God's *perspective*. In the light of eternity, everything but life in Christ fades in importance. God leads us to view others with compassion and care.

... Just summon strength God put *inside*. By the power of the Holy Spirit, God's people are given inner strength and blessed with the resources mentioned in these Bible verses.

... Without the use of God's gift—*rest*. God made us to need rest for renewal and health.

... God's gift of humor helps you *smile!* Proverbs 17:22 reminds us, "A cheerful heart is good medicine." The joy that results from knowing Jesus as our Savior is reflected in our outlook on life. The very act of smiling reduces stress and warms the hearts of those around us. Looking for the humor in a trying situation helps us keep things in perspective and lightens our mood.

4. As we view our world through the perspective of the cross, living in Christ (Colossians 2:6–7), the Holy Spirit empowers us to live in forgiveness and love.

5. Encourage individuals or small groups to complete the paraphrase, not feeling limited by style or format.

Certainty

Emphasize again the vastness of the spiritual and emotional resources made available to us through the ever-flowing fountain of Christ's love.

Prayer

Conclude by joining in the words of benediction.

SESSION 4

You and Me, Lord, ...

as I become spiritually challenged!

Reflection: Christ is the Answer. What is the Question?

Begin by reading the opening paragraphs. Pray responsively the words of the psalmist, who brings his uncertainties to God, trusting Him for help and hope.

Pardon for the Past

1. Contrast the human attitudes with that of Jesus as indicated in the passages from Scripture. He did not question His role or position. He humbly accepted God's will and put Himself into His heavenly Father's hands. He did this willingly out of love for us.

2. Ask class members to read the letters from the three women. Perhaps at the conclusion of the session, you may want to divide into groups, revisit the three women, and write a response to their questions.

Diane was hurt and frustrated when her plans weren't the same as those God had in mind for her. Emphasize the fact that God remains trustworthy. He does not cause the tragedy, but can work His will in the midst of pain, for our good and the good of His Kingdom.

Carla appears a bit more self-centered in her expectations. The amazing fact is that God does care about the seemingly personal and even trivial aspects of the lives of His children. A reminder to let God be God and trust His timing would be in order.

Lilleth can be given reassurance of the constant presence of God, who has guided her in the earlier stages of her life and is still with her. Emphasize Christ and His Word spoken in truth and purity as the focus of worship. In that context, encourage renewed enthusiasm in worship, no matter what the time or tempo. God can provide wisdom and comfort through His Word, which does not change. (Hebrews 13:8)

3. All three women are affected by fear—fear of being hurt, fear of missing out, fear of losing something. Psalm 56 reminds us that the trust God provides to us frees us from fear. Focusing on Him rather than on our worries can bring peace.

4. a. Jesus' reply to John was a listing of His actions. He provided many examples of His power and providence.

b. Jesus' reply was particularly significant because it provided evidence of the fulfillment of Old Testament prophecy and demonstrated that Jesus is God—the Promised Messiah.

5. Give class members time to recall and share with the group specific ways they too have seen God at work.

6. Ask volunteers to read the summary of problems with which we are beset, and the section which discusses the power God gives us through His forgiving grace.

Power for the Present

1. As you briefly review Job's spiritual challenges, allow time for the group to read the passages and derive information.

a. WHO caused all the trouble? Satan.

b. WHAT were some difficulties? Loss of children and possessions, painful boils and grief.

c. WHO tried to help? Job's wife and three friends, but they were ineffective because they tried to rationalize his difficulties. His wife told him to just give up. His friends tried to convince him God must be punishing some specific sin.

d. WHERE did the blessings originate? From the Lord; they were His to use at His discretion.

e. WHEN would he stop trusting? Never. Comment on the totality of Job's trust. Job realized God's ways may never make sense to him. It didn't matter. He trusted God implicitly,

f. HOW did he feel? Confident. In the context of great calamity Job is led to speak the powerful words of resurrection which have brought comfort to God's people throughout the centuries. He trusted God's plan even though he couldn't understand it.

2. The example of Jesus in the wilderness focuses on His source of strength. The timing was strategic from Satan's viewpoint. Jesus was coming from a spiritual "high"—His Baptism. Satan loves to bring us crashing down to his own level when we are feeling particularly close to our Father. Also, Jesus had been fasting. He may have been physically weak and vulnerable.

a. Discuss the value and power of God's Word as a weapon against the devil's tactics. See also Ephesians 6:10–17.

b. Share times when prayer has been particularly helpful in the lives of class members. The Scripture verses assure us that God personally knows our thoughts, our needs, and even helps us to pray.

c. As angels ministered to Jesus, so God supplies us with healing and renewal.

d. Discuss the value of Christian friends for support and comfort.

3. God is there to watch over and support us. He is holding on to us at our right hand. We may face troubles, but they will not overpower us.

Promise for the Future

Bring a piece of woven material to class if possible, as an example of the warp and woof which make up the completed design. Read the paragraphs and discuss the importance of knowing who, rather than why and how.

Certainty

Read this summarizing paragraph. Suggest that individuals highlight a key sentence of their own choosing.

Prayer

Lead the group in prayer or encourage group members to pray extemporaneously about their personal concerns. Emphasize Romans 8:38–39 and the fact that nothing can separate us from God's love.

SESSION 5

You and Me, Lord, ...

as I seek new opportunities to serve You!

Reflection: No Strings Attached

Read the introductory paragraphs and pray the psalm selection.

Pardon for the Past

1. Give the group a few moments to complete their lists and to indicate their feelings about these commitments. Most people are involved in a variety of projects, some of which they truly enjoy, some of which they do because they have to.

2. Discuss the attitudes listed. Point out that there is not necessarily a right or wrong response. We will not feel excited by every task brought before us. Doing what needs to be done is not necessarily bad; we depend on and appreciate people who take responsibility for unpleasant tasks. And it is important to recognize what we cannot or should not do because of a lack of ability, time, or interest. Also, be careful not to judge those who are reluctant to become involved in outside commitments. For some, taking care of themselves and their family may be a full time and worthwhile responsibility. Then note God's focus on the heart; perhaps we too can consider a heart-check.

3. Consider how much of what we do is motivated by a sense of duty or guilt. Is there a relationship between why we do a task and how we feel about the task? Read the vignettes and discuss the feelings living under the Law evoked in the examples listed.

John operated out of a sense of duty and obligation, but his schedule of misplaced priorities took valuable time and energy that could have been used in more personal ways to accomplish the same goal.

Shannon served out of guilt. Her self-imposed "penance" actually resulted in a "repeat offense" of being too busy to spend time with a family member, this time, her husband.

Rosie's martyrlike attitude resulted in feelings of resentment and anger as she took on an obligation for which she really was not qualified. If she had channeled her energies into a different direction, she would still have been busy, but with a cheerful spirit.

4. Romans 7:5–6 points out that anything we do that is not the result of God's grace and power at work in us cannot fulfill the Law and is, ultimately, sin. (See also Isaiah 64:6.) But, as God's children, we don't have to live like that any more. We are "Spirit-powered" to serve joyfully and effectively. We have been set free to serve one another in love.

5. Jesus' blood has set us free from the Law's bonds so that we may now serve God. All we do for others, we do for the Lord and for His glory. Our lives become lives of service and worship to and through Him. God says in Matthew 25:21, "Well done, good and faithful servant!" because He looks at our acts of service in the light of Christ's perfect servanthood.

Power for the Present

1. a. Ruth served her mother-in-law, Naomi, by being faithful to her and by providing food gleaned from the fields. Her role expanded as she became the wife of Boaz, and an ancestor of King David and of Jesus. God blessed and prepared her for service through her experience in a Hebrew home, and by nurturing her attitudes of loyalty and diligence. Her motivation was love.

b. Hannah served her son, Samuel, and Eli, the priest, by dedicating Samuel to the Lord and following through on her vow. She faithfully visited Samuel and provided him with clothing and support. God was working through her perseverance at prayer and her long wait for Samuel's birth to develop trust and thankfulness in her heart. Again, love was the motivation.

c. Tabitha (Dorcas) gave clothing to the poor. She served through her God-given gifts of sewing skills and a giving nature. God's love for her in Christ Jesus motivated her to love others, and, in so doing, to witness her faith in her Savior. Her resurrected life was a witness to her whole community of God's power.

d. Lydia was a worshiper of God, but learned from Paul specifically about her salvation in Christ. She showed hospitality to Paul and his group and opened her home to them. Her skills and contacts as a business person provided her with a home and income which she used in support of God's messengers. God's hand was at work in this. She was motivated by faith, which the Holy Spirit placed in her heart.

e. Aquila and Priscilla were co-workers of the apostle Paul. They offered the gift of hospitality, helped Paul support himself in the tent-making industry, and studied the Scriptures with him so they too could share the Gospel in its truth and purity. They were responsible for instructing Apollos, who became another proclaimer of the Gospel. God was at work developing not only their tent-making skills (which provided the original contact and support for Paul's influence in their lives), but also their ability to share the Gospel message. Their love for the Lord became evident as a motive for their service.

f. Encourage the members of the class to tell about modern-day people who also serve faithfully. In this discussion, always give the glory to God.

2. As we struggle with decisions of where we can best serve, we are encouraged by Christ's great blessings of *peace* and *joy*.

Promise for the Future

1. Philippians 2:5–11 emphasizes Jesus' humility and obedience to God's will. He came to earth as a human being, enduring poverty and menial tasks (even washing feet). He suffered and died a painful and humiliating death. He humbly did this for us and leads us to respond joyfully in service to Him. Just as God has power to use imperfect things such as a donkey, feed box, and rocks for His purposes, He can also use us imperfect people to carry out His plan and purpose.

2. Discuss areas of service in which these lists may stimulate interest and potential. Consider the possibility that we look for *new* areas of service rather than *additional* ones, to revive the spark of joy in what we do.

3. Invite volunteers to read their prayers as part of the closing activities.

Certainty

Read this summary statement aloud as a proclamation of God's love to us.

Prayer

After reading several of the psalm verses, close with a favorite song of joy-filled praise.

SESSION 6

You and Me, Lord, ...

as I celebrate relationships blessed by You!

Reflection: You and Us Together, Lord

As you read the opening paragraphs, you may want to also read 1 John 4:11–12, 15–16 to expand on the concept that God's love is the basis for our relationship with Him and with others.

Pardon for the Past

1. Allow a few moments for participants to complete the acrostic, which might include words such as:

Forgiving
humoR
kInd
Enthusiastic
patieNt
Defender

2. In small groups, encourage participants to share experiences regarding friendship. Allow about 5–8 minutes. Be sure everyone who wants to has a chance to participate.

3. Gather as a group again and continue reading the paragraphs that follow. The disciples referred to are a-Peter, b-Thomas, c-James and John, and d-Judas.

4. Sin corrupts relationships between people just as it corrupts our relationship with God. God sent Christ to reconcile (reunite, make peace, bring together, restore) us to Himself. Christ has restored our relationship by forgiving our sins so that we may be the people of God. Forgiveness and love are also the keys to all human ties.

Power for the Present

1. Jesus chose us to belong to Him on the basis of grace alone, not because of our own efforts. Friendship with Christ is a privilege—He has lifted us up and has called us His own (John 17:20, 24). He desires that we show love to one another.

2. a. The covenant between David and Jonathan was a mutual one—a bilateral agreement.

b. Jonathan bestowed upon David the symbols of his princely rank. He set aside his position and put this relationship on equal footing. True friendship supercedes all rank and position. It is based on mutual love and respect. Both gave help as needed according to their ability. They did not keep track of who gave more.

c. Jonathan defended and spoke well of David.

d. David's commitment was long-term, extending after Jonathan's death to his son.

e. God's covenant is unique because it is entirely unilateral. He loves and forgives us solely according to His grace and mercy, regardless of our behavior or attitude. Our redemption was His idea. He promised it and brought it about. Jesus not only risked His life,

He gave it up for us. He cares for us even as we continue to sin. God's covenant with us is truly eternal; we will live with Him forever in heaven.

3. a. Continue reading and discussing the material as directed.

b. Encourage participants to someday soon share the chosen Scripture or prayer with that particular friend.

c. Christians can share their most precious gift with non-Christian friends by sharing God's love with them as they lead them to their Savior.

d. The relationship between fellow Christians is a distinct blessing. People who have the same "Best Friend" (Jesus) also have a special relationship with each other. They can forgive each other freely because they know that they, themselves, live in Christ's forgiveness.

Coming together for corporate worship is a particular blessing for believers who are friends. Together we confess our sins and receive the assurance of absolution. Together we receive the blessings of the sacraments. (Note that the Lord's Supper is also called "Communion," emphasizing the fellowship between communicants as members of the body of Christ as well as the union between God and man.) In corporate worship God's people respond together to His Word and encourage each other in songs of praise.

Promise for the Future

You may want to work in groups and then combine lists derived from these encouraging words of Scripture. (Speaking of *encouraging,* you may want to add 1 Thessalonians 5:11 to your list.)

Certainty

After you read the summary of this lesson, you may also want to consider together a summary of this course as a whole.

Prayer

Close with a celebration of blessings we share in Christ.